Orthodoxy for Children

Vladimir Luchaninov

God

**Illustrations by
Ekaterina Golovanova**

Grand Rapids · Exaltation Press · 2019

Copyright © 2019 Exaltation Press

Author: Vladimir Luchaninov
Illustrator: Ekaterina Golovanova
Translator: Fr. John Hogg

"God"
      This book is designed to help young children begin to reflect on the world around and inside themselves and help them begin to reflect on God and His relationship to us and the world around us.

All rights reserved. This book or any portion thereof may not be reproduced or used in any manner whatsoever without the express written permission of the publisher except for the use of brief quotations in a book review.

Translated from the original "О Боге" by Nikea Press, Copyright © Trading house «NIKEA», www.Nikeabooks.ru

ISBN: 978-1-950067-11-4 (Paperback)

Edited by Cynthia Hogg

First printing edition 2019

Exaltation Press
Grand Rapids, MI

www.ExaltationPress.com

For bulk orders, please contact editor@exaltationpress.com.

Table of Contents

THE WORLD AROUND YOU 4

THE WORLD INSIDE YOU 6

THE OMNIPOTENCE OF GOD 8

THE LOVE OF GOD 10

GOD IS ETERNAL 12

THE CREATION OF THE WORLD 14

THE FIRST PEOPLE 18

HOW EVIL ENTERED THE WORLD 20

THE FIRST PEOPLE'S MISTAKE 22

THE HISTORY OF MANKIND 24

GOD COMES TO SAVE MANKIND: JESUS CHRIST 26

THE RESURRECTION OF CHRIST 28

GOD AND US 30

THE WAY TO THE FATHER 32

THE WORLD AROUND YOU

The sun warms the earth and the rain quenches its thirst. The earth gives us everything we need to live. How wonderfully everything is arranged! It is all wise and beautiful. There are immense seas and oceans, rivers and lakes, and what diverse animals live there! Giant whales, intelligent dolphins, funny-looking octopuses, and so many different kinds of fish. Eagles fly over mountaintops and valleys and the lyrical sound of the birds rings out among the green leaves. In shady groves of trees, in thick forests, and in the dense jungles, each animal finds itself a home and food to sustain itself. Everything in our world is rational. Everything makes sense.

And if we look up into the night sky, we see millions of stars smiling at us, shining in the immense, dark, heavenly dome. The starry sky is endless, wondrous, and mysterious.

The Starry Sky and the Conscience

"Two things fill my soul with endless reverence and amazement – the starry sky above me and the moral law within me."

Immanuel Kant,
scientist and philosopher

5 God

THE WORLD INSIDE YOU

The mysterious, endless sky is like your soul. Isn't it amazing that you exist? You live, think, and dream. You can laugh and cry, be silly, and sometimes very serious. Every day, you want to learn something new. Where did the world come from? Why am I in the world? Why am I alive? Is life a gift from someone? Then who do I say "thank you" to?

The One who gave you all of this is called "God."

We call Him the Creator, the Lord, the Almighty, because everything is within His power. We also turn to Him more simply, calling Him our "Heavenly Father," since we are all His children.

It was God who created our world and who gave you life and an eternal soul which is as boundless as the starry sky or the whole enormous Universe.

When the soul sees the Lord, how meek and humble He is, then the soul itself is completely humbled and wants nothing more than the humility of Christ. No matter how long that soul lives on this earth, it will always desire and seek out that incomprehensible humility, which is unforgettable. O Lord, how much you love mankind!

St. Silouan the Athonite

THE OMNIPOTENCE OF GOD

If you want to draw a tree, you have to take a piece of paper and pencils or markers. You need to picture what you want to draw. Even then, it's not clear if it will turn out well the first time. Now imagine – nothing hinders God. He creates everything out of nothing. For Him, there is no difference between thought and action. Distances don't exist for Him. God is with you right now and at the same time with every person in every country, city, and village. He is with adults and children, with the good and even with the wicked. He is always ready to embrace us and He wants each person to enter the path of goodness and love. For God Himself is Love.

> With our mind, we can't even understand how the sun was made. When we ask God to tell us how He made the sun, we receive the answer clearly in our soul, "Humble yourself and you will not only know the sun but also its creator."
>
> *St. Silouan the Athonite*

9 God

THE LOVE OF GOD

God has put within you the need to love. First of all, to love those closest to you – your parents, siblings, relatives, friends – in a word, all of those who are near you. But He also wants you to love everyone, each person. That is why it feels so pleasant to do good to others, even to strangers.

You also have in your soul the desire to be loved by others. You want them to understand you and not to wrong you. When others do wrong you, you know something isn't right because what they're doing is not according to love! That feeling helps you to understand that if you wrong your neighbors, they will also be upset, so you shouldn't hurt them.

God gave us love, He put it in our hearts, because He created us for joy and for eternal life. You already have that love in your heart. It is very important that you feel it, preserve it, and give it to those around you.

The Two Greatest Commandments

You shall love the Lord your God with all your heart and with all your soul and with all your mind. This is the great and first commandment. And a second is like it: You shall love your neighbor as yourself.

The Gospel of Matthew 22:37-40

GOD IS ETERNAL

There was never a time when God didn't exist. In fact, time itself was created by God and He was before all time. As He rules our world, as He knows you and watches how you grow, He Himself abides in eternity where there is neither beginning nor end.

Perhaps you have noticed that time seems to flow differently depending on your mood. When you're happy, time seems to fly by and when you're sad, time seems to get stuck and frozen in place. There isn't a difference if you look at the clock. Rather, it is in your soul. Your soul belongs to eternity, where there is both joy and progress towards perfection.

13 God

THE CREATION OF THE WORLD

Before He created our world, the Lord created the angels, who are both wondrous and good. They are His servants. They are invisible to the human eye but our hearts can sometimes feel their presence and their help. Each of us has a guardian angel. You have one, too.

God created the whole universe, the galaxies, the planets, and our earth out of nothing. The Lord separated the dry land from the water and the earth brought forth grass, flowers, and trees. The plants filled the atmosphere with oxygen which we need to live. God lit up the sky with stars and at His command, the planets began their cosmic dance. The two great lights, the sun and the moon, take turns lighting the earth, day and night. He filled the oceans, seas, and rivers with their mysterious inhabitants.

Birds appeared in the sky, filling the newborn world with gladness and singing, as if they were flowers flying in the clear sky. A great variety of animals settled all over the dry land.

God

A Prayer to Your Guardian Angel

Be merciful to me, O holy angel of the Lord, my guardian, and do not leave me but rather enlighten me with the unapproachable light and make me worthy of the Kingdom of Heaven.

THE FIRST PEOPLE

Afterward, the Lord created the very first human being. His name is Adam. He was supposed to be the steward of all creation. The Lord breathed into him the Breath of Life. That gave Adam freedom and rationality.

God brought all the animals to Adam and he gave each of them a name. That is how mankind became the king of this world.

The Lord put Adam into a deep sleep and when he awoke, he saw a beautiful young woman. He called her Eve. Adam and Eve became the first couple, the first family, the mother and father of all the people of the world. Their blood flows in each of us. All of us, even though we have different colored skin, speak different languages, and live on different continents, are their children. That is why we say that all human beings are brothers and sisters.

Adam and Eve lived and worked in the Garden of Eden, which they called Paradise. Since God trusted them with everything, He expected them to trust Him as well, especially when it came to the mysterious tree, the Tree of the Knowledge of Good and Evil, that grew in the garden. They were forbidden to eat its fruit.

19 God

HOW EVIL ENTERED THE WORLD

The happiness that the young world enjoyed was shattered by a proud angel named Lucifer. He envied God. Imagine it. It would be like if there were a generous king who showed mercy to his servant, sending him gifts. However, in spite of the many gifts, that servant began to hate his benefactor for being richer and wiser than he was and decided to try to seize everything for himself.

Lucifer was embittered. Envy ate him up from the inside and then broke out to the world around him. That is how evil first appeared. From then on, that fallen angel has been called Satan and he tries to ruin everything that God gives us. The word "Satan" means "opponent" since, in his madness, he tries to oppose the Almighty God. Among the angels, there were some others who were unfaithful to God and became Satan's slaves, carrying evil within themselves. It was easier for them to take away the Kingdom from mankind than to fight against God directly. Satan planned to use trickery to lead mankind to make a fatal mistake.

> "Whoever carries in himself the peace of the Holy Spirit pours out that peace on others but whoever carries in himself a spirit of evil pours out that evil on others as well."
>
> St. Silouan the Athonite

THE FIRST PEOPLE'S MISTAKE

Taking on the form of a serpent, Satan persuaded Eve to disobey God and taste the forbidden fruit. He said that when they tasted it, Adam and Eve would become powerful and since God didn't want that to happen, He forbade them to eat from the Tree of the Knowledge of Good and Evil. But that was a lie.

At that moment, the first woman did not remember the goodness of God. She wanted to be powerful. Unfortunately, that happens sometimes. Eve plucked some fruit and began to eat. Adam did not even try to stop her but rather followed her example. The Devil gloated that he had achieved his goal...

At that moment, evil entered the human heart like an infectious disease. Adam and Eve changed significantly. The royal dignity they had had melted away like ice beneath the hot sun and instead they were confused and afraid. All of the animals, horrified that the order God had created was gone, no longer obeyed mankind. The perfection of God's creation was broken.

Like a drop of black paint falling into a cup of clear water instantly makes the water gray, the truth in the hearts of Adam and Eve was mixed with deception. They could no longer live in Paradise. Ever since, people have had to make the difficult choice between good and evil

Good and Evil

The Devil sowed evil in the hearts of mankind. Ever since, all sorts of suffering takes place in this world. The strong hurt the weak, wars bring sorrow and destruction...

But evil can never defeat good because God, who is good, rules over all and so goodness is endued with great power.

and earthly life has become a time of testing and trial. Each of us dies, but only in body. Our souls remain eternal and immortal.

THE HISTORY OF MANKIND

God doesn't only know what has been but also what will be. Before the creation of the world, He knew that humanity might make a mistake and so He prepared for us a way to correct that mistake.

To comfort Adam and Eve, the Lord foretold the birth of a Savior, Who would defeat the devil, bring us back to God, and once again give us the gift of eternal happiness.

Humanity still had to undergo many trials. The earth no longer obeyed them. The wild animals were now dangerous. Even the seemingly insignificant bugs now started to bite human beings, as if in revenge.

Years passed, then centuries and millennia. Over time, there were more and more people on the earth and more things to worry about, too. Families grew into tribes, tribes into peoples, and peoples into large civilizations. Human beings, endowed with the gift of creativity, began to subdue the world around them. They made it more comfortable for themselves but that didn't mean there was more goodness or happiness. People were born and died but they did not find comfort in eternity because they had lost their connection with the Source of Life. The memory of Adam and Eve was disappearing and many even forgot about God.

Only one people held on strongly to the memory of God. This was the Israelites. They knew that the Savior, promised by God, would be born from their people. He would restore the blessedness of Paradise and would renew the corrupted world. God spoke to the people of Israel through the prophets who foretold that the Savior would come into the world in a miraculous way. He would be born of a Virgin whose soul was radiant and pure.

GOD COMES TO SAVE MANKIND: JESUS CHRIST

The Holy Spirit descended on a young Israelite girl named Mary and in an incomprehensible way, a great mystery took place inside of her: Divinity was united with humanity. For nine months, the Virgin Mary carried inside of her the miraculous Divine Child, the Son of God. When He was born, Mary gave Him the name Jesus, the name that the Archangel Gabriel had told her. He had told her in advance about the wonder that would take place, that she would give birth to the Savior of the world.

This happened two thousand years ago. The birth of Jesus Christ is so important that we even figure out what year it is by counting from His birth, which was the beginning of a new era.

While Jesus was little, He lived with His mother and her protector, Joseph. Once He had grown up, He went out and began to serve people. Divine power and love rang out in His words, in the help He gave to those who were suffering, in how He healed the sick and raised the dead. Jesus taught boundless mercy and forgiveness and He taught us to love our enemies.

People came from all over to see Him, asking for His help, wanting to become His disciples. After all, our souls are created by God and so they perceive Him and long for Him. However, people who have forgotten love and goodness often cannot bear God's divine light and try to hide from it. The teachers of the Jewish people at the time were like that. They looked for a way to kill Him. The Son of God, who came to save mankind, was condemned by them to death. They mocked Him and then crucified Him on the Cross.

The Holy Trinity

We are unable to imagine God or describe what He is like but we know that He is the Holy Trinity. There is only one God but in that Unity, there are Three Persons who abide in harmony and love. The Father, the Son, and the Holy Spirit. Although it is not exactly the same, it might help to imagine the sun. The physical sun, its rays of light, and its warmth are distinguishable from each other but at the same time, there is only one sun.

THE RESURRECTION OF CHRIST

It was on the Cross, however, that all humanity was saved. The Son of God took on Himself the sins of the whole world. He forgave those who crucified Him. He showed people His love and proved that He was ready to endure to the end for our salvation. They killed Him but death was not able to swallow the Creator of the world. On the third day, Christ rose from the dead. He broke the power of the devil and freed the souls of Adam and Eve from hell, as well as the souls of all those languishing there.

By His Resurrection, Christ once again united humanity with God and opened the way for us to eternal blessedness. Jesus Christ, the Son of God, ascended to His Heavenly Father and the Holy Spirit descended on the disciples of Jesus, the Church, which He founded on the earth. Through Jesus Christ, the earth was once more joined to heaven, time was joined to eternity, and we, human beings, were reunited with our God.

> Whoever eats My flesh and drinks My blood has eternal life, and I will raise him up at the last day. For My flesh is food indeed, and My blood is drink indeed. He who eats My flesh and drinks My blood abides in Me, and I in him.
>
> *Gospel of John 6:54-56*

29 God

GOD AND US

As human beings, we live our lives and then, when we get older, our bodies slowly lose their physical strength and we die. Sometimes, people even die while they are still young, at the height of their physical strength. However, at the moment of death, our souls fly like a bird to God in eternity. They go where there is no time, where no one will ever die again. There, Jesus Christ greets us, and all people who love each other remain together forever, like children in the home of their Heavenly Father. In Heaven, there will be no boredom, hurt, or pain. There is only endless joy, action, life, love, and progress towards perfection. This happiness, however, is only revealed to those do not have evil thoughts in their hearts. Evil cannot enter the eternal Kingdom of Christ.

Here on the earth, the devil is still active. He may have been defeated and lost his former power but he is still evil and cunning. Our faith in Jesus Christ deprives him of his power over us. All the evil that Satan or mankind has sown in the world will eventually be overcome by God's goodness. In eternity, we will understand many things that are unclear to us now and will find the answers to our unanswered questions.

Have you ever noticed that when you do something unkind, even if no one else knows about it, your heart gets heavy and your joy disappears? Something inside you makes you want to admit what you did and ask forgiveness. When you finally make up your mind and do it, your heart becomes light and peaceful, as if a weight fell from you. If you talk to Christ in prayer and try not to do things that are wrong, your soul will feel that lightness more and more over time. The closer we are to Him, the more joy we have in our hearts and the more happiness in our lives.

THE WAY TO THE FATHER

From the very beginning, it is very important for us to open our whole hearts to God and to try not to let evil thoughts and feelings enter them.

When a young tree is bent towards the ground it is easy to straighten it so that its trunk grows straight up, stretching towards the sun. If, however, the tree continues to grow while still crooked, no gardener is able to straighten it. The human soul is somewhat like a tree. While you are young and full of strength, it is easier to get rid of your heart's tendency towards evil. The more you get used to it, however, the harder it is to get rid of it.

The way to God is not always easy. We must strive to reach His light through love and through overcoming our evil thoughts. Often, this is a fight that lasts our whole life long. Everyone likes books, movies, and cartoons about real heroes. Sometimes it seems like there is no hope, that they cannot overcome the villains, but they ultimately win in the end. The same thing is true in our lives. We need to have faith in victory and not give up. The Lord Himself will help you in everything for He is the one who wants to give you the Eternal Kingdom of joy and gladness.

> Once, people brought children to see Christ. There were many children and they ran about, making noise. The disciples decided not to let these people with their children see Jesus. They were afraid there would be chaos and that the children would disturb Jesus with their games. Jesus, however, said, "Let the little children come to me and do not hinder them for theirs is the Kingdom of God."

www.ingramcontent.com/pod-product-compliance
Lightning Source LLC
Chambersburg PA
CBHW051350110526
44591CB00025B/2963